A Note to Parents and T

DK READERS is a compelling
beginning readers, designed in
leading literacy experts.

Beautiful illustrations and superb full-colour
photographs combine with engaging, easy-to-read
stories to offer a fresh approach to each subject in
the series. Each DK READER is guaranteed to
capture a child's interest while developing his or
her reading skills, general knowledge and love
of reading.

The five levels of DK READERS are aimed at
different reading abilities, enabling you to choose
the books that are exactly right for your child:

Pre-level 1 – Learning to read
Level 1 – Beginning to read
Level 2 – Beginning to read alone
Level 3 – Reading alone
Level 4 – Proficient readers

The "normal" age at which a child begins to read can
be anywhere from three to eight years old, so these levels
are only a general guideline.

No matter which level
you select, you can be
sure that you are
helping your child
learn to read, then
read to learn!

Penguin
Random
House

For Dorling Kindersley
Editor Kate Simkins
Senior Designer David McDonald
Slipcase Designer Stefan Georgiou
Designer Nick Avery
Pre-Production Producer Kavita Varma
Senior Producer Alex Bell
Managing Editor Sadie Smith
Managing Art Editor Ron Stobbart
Creative Manager Sarah Harland
Art Director Lisa Lanzarini
Publisher Julie Ferris
Publishing Director Simon Beecroft

Reading Consultant Cliff Moon, M.Ed.

For Lucasfilm
Art Editor Iain R. Morris
Senior Editor Jonathan W. Rinzler
Continuity Supervisor Leland Chee

This edition published in 2016
First published in Great Britain in 2005
by Dorling Kindersley Limited,
80 Strand, London, WC2R 0RL

Slipcase UI: 001-305124-Oct/16

Page design copyright © 2016 Dorling Kindersley Limited.
A Penguin Random House Company

© and TM 2016 LUCASFILM LTD.

All rights reserved. Without limiting the rights under
the copyright reserved above, no part of this publication may
be reproduced, stored in or introduced into a retrieval system, or
transmitted, in any form, or by any means (electronic, mechanical,
photocopying, recording, or otherwise), without the prior written
permission of the copyright owner.

A CIP catalogue record for this book
is available from the British Library

ISBN: 978-1-4053-1001-7

Printed in China.

www.starwars.com
www.dk.com

A WORLD OF IDEAS:
SEE ALL THERE IS TO KNOW

DK READERS

BEGINNING TO READ

1

STAR WARS

What is a Wookiee?

Written by Laura Buller and Kate Simkins

My name
is C-3PO.

I am a droid.
I am a talking
machine.

I live far, far away in space.
Lots of creatures live here.
I will be telling you
about some of them.

Space

Some creatures in *Star Wars* are aliens.

Aliens are not human.
There are lots of different aliens.

Humans also live here –
my friend Padmé (PAD-MAY) is
a human.

This is my friend R2-D2.
He is a droid too.

R2-D2 likes talking.
His voice sounds like
whistles and beeps, but
I can understand him.

R2-D2 is a clever
little machine.
He has all sorts
of useful tools.
He can fix anything!

Tool

Meet Chewbacca.

He is a tall,
furry alien
called
a Wookiee.

He is the best friend of Han Solo, who is a human.
They fly a spaceship together.

Sometimes,
I ride with them!

Spaceship

Now say hello
to Jar Jar Binks.

He is a friendly
alien.

Jar Jar comes from
an underwater city.
On land, Jar Jar is always
falling over!

He uses his long tongue
to catch food to eat.

Let's visit Watto's shop.

Watto is a blue alien.
He has a bad temper.
Watto flies about
using the wings on his back.

He sells bits of old machines
called junk.

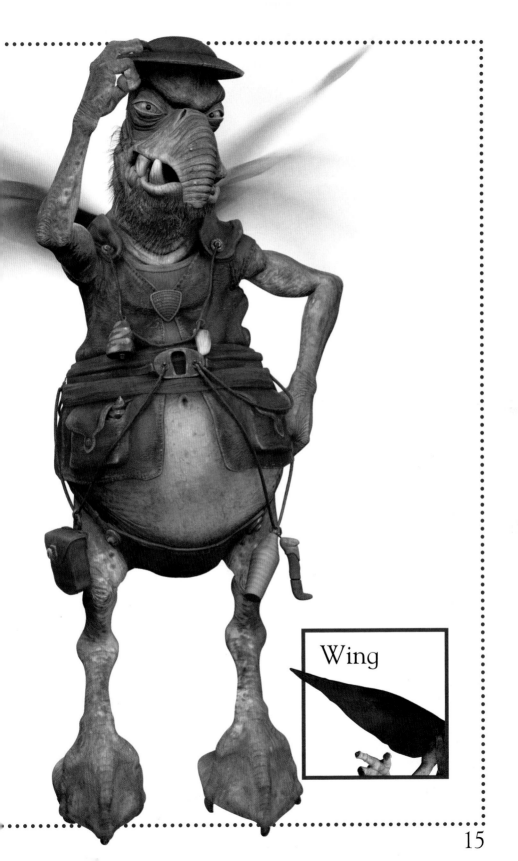

Wing

15

Now it's time
to meet Sebulba
(SEE-BUL-BAH).

This nasty alien races in a vehicle called a Podracer. He likes to go fast.

Podracer

Sebulba will do anything to win. He will even throw things at other Podracers!

Pit droids fix the Podracers.
They are very useful and
can carry heavy things.

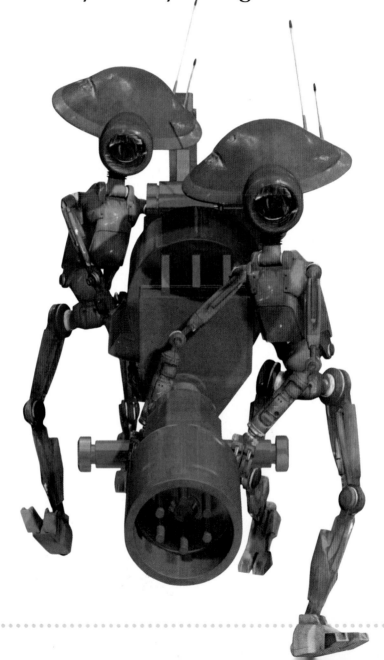

Pit droids sometimes
get into trouble.
There is one way to stop them.
Tap them on the nose
and they fold up.

Jabba the Hutt is a nasty alien.
He has a fat body and a long tail.
His body is covered in sticky slime.

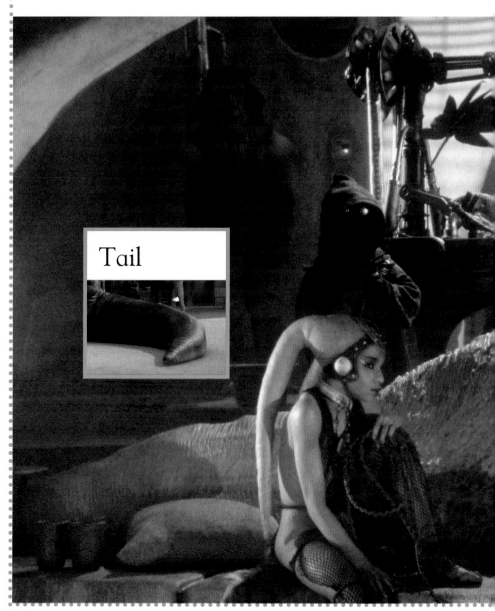

Tail

Jabba's eyes are red and yellow
and his breath is smelly.
Don't get too near him!

Let's visit Dexter Jettster's restaurant.

This friendly alien has four arms. He cooks the food at Dexter's Dine

Dexter knows lots of things.
What shall we ask him?

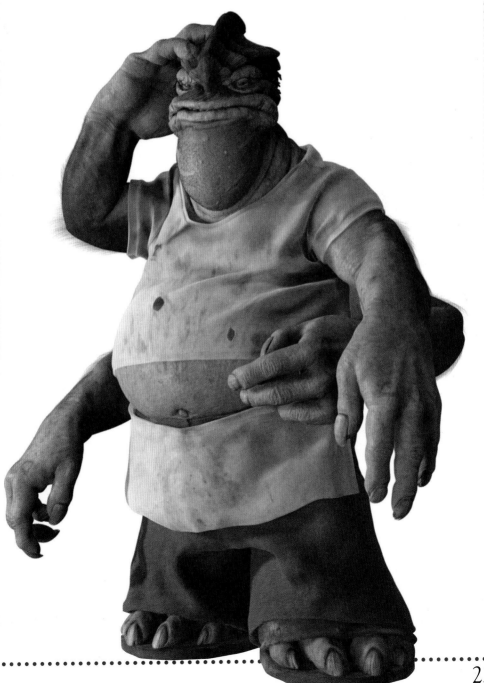

These creatures
are lizard keepers.

They live
in big holes
in the ground.

Sometimes, the lizard keepers ride around on giant lizards. The lizards are good at jumping and climbing.

Jawas are small creatures
with shiny yellow eyes.

Their faces
are hidden under
the hoods of
their brown cloaks.

Hood

These little aliens
find droids and
bits of machines to sell.

Once, they even sold
R2-D2!

If we go deep into the forest,
we may meet the Ewoks.

Ewoks are small, furry creatures.
They live in houses
that they build high up
in the trees.

Forest

Yoda is very old and very wise.
He has green skin and
big, pointy ears.

No one knows what kind
of creature he is or
where he comes from.

I hope you have enjoyed
learning about the creatures
in *Star Wars.*

Goodbye!

Picture Word List

Space

Podracer

Tool

Tail

Spaceship

Hood

Wing

Forest